One night, Uncle Al, Aunt Lucy, and
I were watching a swimming race on
TV. "Can you swim, Mike?" Uncle Al
asked me.

"Not yet, but I want to learn" I said.

"Mike wants to learn to swim," Uncle Al told my dad. "It's best to learn early, when you're a child. We're too old now."

Dad's voice boomed, "Too OLD to learn? Not me!"

My dad likes to learn new things.

Dad tapped his thumb on his chin.
I knew he was planning something.

A few days later, Dad said, "I signed
Mike up for a swimming class."

"Hooray!" I shouted.

Then Dad smiled. "I signed myself
up, too," he said.

There were six students in the class.
Five were my age. Number six was Dad.
A few kids giggled when they saw my
dad, but that didn't bother him.

Our teacher was named Winny.
Winny showed us the rules of the
pool. "It is unsafe to run. You might
slip."

"Your neck should stick up from the water," Winny said. The water was just under my neck. It was up to Dad's middle.

"Hop over to that deeper spot," Winny said to Dad. Dad hopped.

First we blew bubbles.

"Talk to the fish," said Winny. "Then turn your head. Listen to the fish."

"Talk to the fish, then listen to the fish," she said over and over.

I blew bubbles in the water. Then I breathed in when I turned my head for air.

"SPLOOFLE!" Dad snorted.  "I was
listening to the fish instead of talking!"
he sputtered.  "Show me how to do it
right."  I showed him.

Winny passed out boards. "Kick as
hard as you can!" she said. "Try to get
me wet!" We all tried. The water turned
to foam.

Dad had no trouble splashing. He
kicked up so much water that Winny's
hair was dripping. "That's all for now,"
Winny said.

When we were getting dressed, Dad
said, "Well, I learned a few things. How
about you?"

"It was a good start," I said.

I liked swimming class. It was
fun. We jumped in. We bobbed up
and down.

We helped each other float on
our backs.

"I'm a little heavy," Dad said. "I
think I need another pair of helpers."

We were in the locker room. Roy
said to me, "Your dad is the best!"

"He is?" I asked. I thought Dad's
swimming still needed work.

In the next class, we floated face down. I wished I could float like that for a million years.

After a while, Dad got the hang of floating, too.

Winny showed us how to paddle like a dog.  I paddled in a big circle.  Dad stayed in one spot.  "I'm paddling like a dog!" he panted.

Winny tossed a ring into the pool.
It settled to the bottom.

"Can you get the ring?" she asked.

It took me three tries to grab the
ring. I popped to the top and held it up.

Then it was Dad's turn. He had the
ring in a flash. Dad was better than
the rest of us at this game.

Then Winny taught us how to do
the crawl.

"Move your arms like this," she said.

"Kick your legs like this," she said.

"Move your head like this," she said.

"Why are you waving your arms
like that?" Mom asked Dad.
"I'm doing the crawl," he said.

The weeks went by fast. At our last
class, we took a test.

"Swim from this end to that end,"
Winny said. I did the crawl from one
end to the other.

Then it was Dad's turn.
"Swim, Dad!" I yelled.
"Swim! Swim!" the other kids yelled.
He made it! "You're the best," I said.

We kept up with our swimming.
One summer day, I saw Dad tap his
chin with his thumb. I knew he was
planning something, but what?

# On My Way
## Practice Reader

**Theme 5**
## Family Time
- Swim, Dad!

ISBN 0-618-08971-3

9 780618 089710

1-43877-**2**

HOUGHTON MIFFLIN